EDGE
BOOKS™

LIBRARY OF WEIRD

THE WORLD'S
STRANGEST
FOODS

by Alicia Z. Klepeis

raintree

Raintree is an imprint of Capstone Global Library Limited, a company incorporated in England and Wales having its registered office at 7 Pilgrim Street, London, EC4V 6LB – Registered company number: 6695582

www.raintree.co.uk
myorders@raintree.co.uk

ISBN 978 1 4062 9210 7
18 17 16 15
10 9 8 7 6 5 4 3 2 1

British Library Cataloguing in Publication Data
A full catalogue record for this book is available from the British Library.

Editorial Credits
Aaron Sautter, editor; Kyle Grenz, designer; Charmaine Whitman and Katy LaVigne, production designers; Pam Mitsakos, media researcher; Kathy McColley, production specialist

Photo Credits
Art Explosion Image Library: 17 (top), 26; Dreamstime: Kmitu, 21 (bottom), Ragsac19, 6, Seanjeeves, back cover, Viktorfischer, 13 (top); Getty Images: Science Source/Daniele Pellegrini, 7, Photodisc, 29 (bottom); Landov: MOHAMED NURELDIN ABDALLAH, 23, KIM KYUNG-HOON, 24, EPA/SHERWIN, 4–5; Shutterstock: 33333, 14, ChameleonsEye, 29 (top), Fotokon, 20, 9george, 13 (bottom), Jubal Harshaw, 8, Humannet, 22, insima, 15, Kenishirotie, 9, Andrew Lam, cover, Malgorzata Kistryn, 28, Nancy Kennedy, 27, picturepartners, 17, Glenn R. Specht-grs photo, 16, Piotr Wawrzyniuk, 12, zcw, 5 (inset); Wikimedia: Andrew Bogot, 25, Chris 73, 18, ComQuat, 11, Jonkerz, 21 (top), Shardan, 19, Sputnikcccp, 10

Design Elements
Shutterstock: AridOcean, KID_A (throughout)

Printed and bound in China.

CONTENTS

FREAKY, FAR-OUT FOODS

Can you remember the last slice of pizza you ate? The crispy crust, tangy tomato sauce and melted cheese blended together to make a tasty dinner. Or maybe you recently enjoyed a juicy cheeseburger and some crunchy chips. Now imagine eating a deep-fried tarantula. Does that sound disgusting? You may think so. But people in Cambodia think they're delicious!

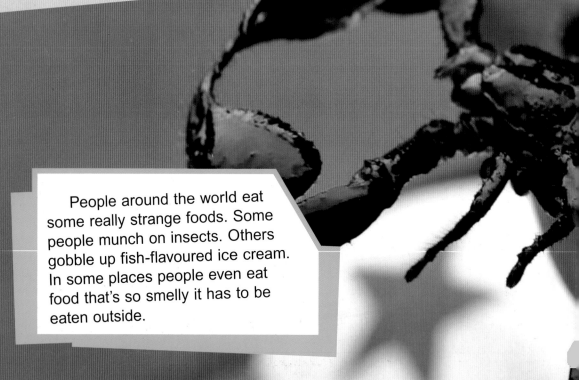

People around the world eat some really strange foods. Some people munch on insects. Others gobble up fish-flavoured ice cream. In some places people even eat food that's so smelly it has to be eaten outside.

Foods that some people think are disgusting may be very appealing to others. For example, you might like crispy chicken strips. But in some parts of the world people actually prefer chicken feet!

We live in a world that offers a variety of strange options. Read on to discover some of the bizarre fo people around the world prefer on their plates.

CHAPTER 1

BIZARRE BREAKFASTS

Do you like cereal, toast or scrambled eggs for breakfast? These foods are probably quite common where you live. But some people like very different options to start their day. Check out these unusual breakfast foods!

MENUDO SOUP

People in Mexico sometimes enjoy menudo soup for breakfast. The chewy, rubbery stuff in the soup is tripe, or cow's stomach. Your teeth will get a workout eating this for breakfast. The soup's meaty broth often contains dried chilli peppers and pigs' feet too.

SCRAPPLE

Some people don't like to waste anything! In parts of the United States, some people use every last part of a pig to make scrapple. Bits of scrap meat are boiled and mixed with cornmeal and spices to form a kind of meat mush. The mush is then formed into a loaf and allowed to cool. People then just cut off a few slices of scrapple and fry them up with their eggs for breakfast!

COW'S BLOOD

Feeling thirsty? The Maasai people in Kenya and Tanzania often start their day by drinking cow's blood. Sometimes they drink it plain. And sometimes they mix the blood with milk. This strange brew is packed with nutrients. For this reason, Maasai women often drink cow's blood after giving birth.

COWS' FEET SOUP

People in the highlands of Ecuador might start their day with a hearty bowl of cows' feet soup. Some all-night restaurants in Quito, Ecuador, specialize in cows' feet soup. Peanut butter and **hominy** are often added to it to give it some texture.

hominy *corn kernels with the hulls removed*

EMU EGGS

If you're hiking in Australia's **outback**, you could try a scrambled emu egg for breakfast. One emu egg is equal to about 10 to 12 chicken eggs, so you might need to share it with some friends. Australia's Arrernte people consider emu eggs a **delicacy**. They sometimes even eat them raw. Fancy a hard-boiled emu egg in the morning? It takes about 1 hour and 45 minutes – not exactly a quick breakfast!

outback *huge area in the middle of Australia that is covered by deserts and rocks*

delicacy *food that is rare and considered to be especially delicious*

LAVERBREAD

Move over, toast and jam! Why not try some tasty seaweed cakes instead? In Wales laverbread is made by cooking laver seaweed and mashing it into a paste. People then mix the paste with ground oats to make laverbread cakes. The seaweed cakes are said to taste salty like the sea. They're part of a traditional Welsh breakfast.

NASI LEMAK

People throughout Southeast Asia begin the day with *nasi lemak*. This Malaysian rice dish is made of rice cooked in coconut milk. In English *nasi lemak* actually means, "rice in cream." It is often served with fried fish, nuts, cucumbers and sometimes an egg.

KOPI LUWAK COFFEE

Drinking coffee is a morning ritual for people around the world. However, some people think *kopi luwak* coffee is special. In parts of Southeast Asia, coffee beans are first eaten and then excreted by cat-like animals called civets. People pick the beans out of the civet poo, clean them up and then grind and brew them. The animals' digestive system is said to take the bitterness out of the beans. Fans say that *kopi luwak* coffee tastes rich and slightly sweet. But this specialized coffee isn't cheap. It often sells for hundreds of pounds per kilogram!

CHAPTER 2

LOONY LUNCHES

All over the world people stop what they're doing and take a break for lunch. Many people grab sandwiches, salads or bowls of soup. But not all lunches are the same. Check out the following bizarre midday meals. You may lose your appetite along the way!

WITCHETTY GRUBS

Desert-dwelling **Aborigines** in Australia often eat witchetty **grubs**. These fat, white grubs are found inside the roots of trees and bushes. They are rich in protein, calcium and iron. Sometimes people eat the nutty-tasting creatures live. But most people grill the fat grubs to make the skins crispy and the insides solid.

Aborigine *people who lived in Australia before European settlers arrived there*

grub *tiny creature that will become an insect; a larva*

MOPANE WORMS

Many people in southern Africa think mopane worms are delicious. People often eat them as a sun-dried snack. They're said to taste like salty crisps. The worms can also be roasted or cooked in stews. Another popular way to cook mopane worms is frying them in peanut butter sauce.

FRIED TARANTULAS

In Skuon, Cambodia, people enjoy snacking on fried tarantulas. They're a very popular type of street food. The spiders are fried with salt, sugar and garlic. People enjoy the spiders' crispy outside and gooey middle. The spiders come from a large network of nearby spider holes. Local street merchants sell hundreds of the fried spider snacks every day.

SURSTRÖMMING

Some people in Sweden enjoy eating *surströmming* or "sour herring." Fishermen catch small Baltic herring in the spring and allow them to **ferment** in **brine** for about a month. The fish are then packed into tins and shipped to shops. The fish continue to ferment inside the tins, which begin to bulge. Fans of the sour fish eat it on flat bread with slices of boiled potato and onion. People almost always eat *surströmming* outdoors because of its foul stench!

ferment *undergo a chemical change*
brine *salty water*

BALTIC HERRING

FROG PORRIDGE

Many restaurants and food stands in Singapore offer frog porridge. Frog legs are cooked in sauce and served in a clay pot with rice. People often compare the taste of frog legs to tender chicken. Dried chillies, ginger and spring onions help give frog porridge some kick!

HEAD CHEESE

People in many places like to eat head cheese, which isn't really cheese at all. People first cook down the meat and fat from a pig's or cow's head. Sometimes they throw in the animal's feet, tongue and heart too. The mixture is then pressed into a mould and allowed to cool into a block of meaty **gelatin**. The block is then cut into slices, which are eaten as is or in a sandwich.

gelatin *clear substance made from bones and animal tissue*

DUCK DELICACIES

Duck meat is a popular food for many people around the world. But some people don't let any part of a duck go to waste. In China people enjoy roasted duck hearts, duck feet in mustard sauce and fried duck tongues. Balut is popular in the Philippines. These baby ducks are boiled in their eggshells before they hatch. People eat all of them, including their feathers. Fancy a special French duck dish? Try *foie gras* or "fatty liver," which is made from the livers of fattened ducks.

BALUT

CHAPTER 3

STRANGE SUPPERS

Families everywhere sit down to share evening meals. Some of these suppers would look extremely strange to us, and sometimes they're smelly too. But the following foods really are loved by some people.

ANIMAL HEADS

Do you mind if your food looks at you while you're eating it? People in some parts of the world consider animal heads to be a special treat. In Singapore people enjoy seasoned fish heads. Visitors to the market in Marrakesh, Morocco, can also enjoy boiled sheep's head!

QUAQ

Some people in Arctic regions eat frozen meat called quaq. Common varieties of quaq include caribou, seal, fish and musk ox. The meat is often eaten with a hearty helping of salt. Caribou quaq is similar to very rare roast beef. Arctic **char** quaq is just like sushi, or uncooked fish, apart from the fact that it's frozen.

CARIBOU

MUSK OX

char *type of fish similar to salmon or trout*

FUGU

Some people in Japan enjoy *fugu*, or pufferfish. These funny-looking poisonous fish are an unusual food choice. Only certain parts of the fish can be eaten safely. *Fugu* chefs in Japan are specially trained to safely prepare the fish for eating. These cooks must also be licensed by the government. After all, killing one's customers is not in any chef's best interest.

GUINEA PIGS

Guinea pigs are very popular in Ecuador and Peru – but not as pets. People slow roast them on a barbeque **spit**. They are often served whole with spicy hot pepper sauce. Sometimes guinea pigs are cooked in stews or boiled in soup.

spit *long, pointed rod that holds meat over a fire for cooking*

SLÁTUR

Do you have a strong stomach? You'll need one to make *slátur*, a traditional dish from Iceland. Supermarkets in Iceland sell the necessary ingredients including sheep blood, livers, **suet** and stomachs. Some *slátur* kits also include grains, salt, needles and thread. Why do you need needles and thread? First a sheep's stomach is cut into 4 or 5 pieces. These pieces are then stuffed with the ingredients listed and sewn up at the ends to make sausages.

suet *hard fat from animals that is used in cooking*

SVARTSOPPA

In Sweden people often celebrate St Martin's Day by feasting on *svartsoppa*, or "black soup." The main ingredient of this sweet-and-sour soup is goose blood. The soup also gets its colour from spices and mashed fruits.

KHLII

People in Morocco enjoy camel *khlii*, which is a type of preserved meat. The camel meat is first dried for days under the hot sun. The fat that comes out coats and preserves the meat. Moroccans often add *khlii* to scrambled eggs.

HÁKARL

Did you know that sharks expel urine through their skin? That doesn't bother some people in Iceland who like *hákarl*, or rotting shark meat. To make *hákarl*, Icelanders bury shark meat in beach gravel for three months to filter out the poisons in it. But the meat still smells of urine, ammonia and rotten fish. People then hang up the foul-smelling meat to dry out for five more months before eating it.

KANGAROO

People in Australia like to eat kangaroo meat in many ways. Kangaroo steaks are quite popular. People enjoy several kinds of kangaroo soups and stews as well. One type includes chunks of kangaroo tail!

SCORPIONS

Most people don't eat poisonous creatures. However, many people in China eat cooked scorpions. Cooking them removes the poison from their stingers. Cooked scorpion meat is said to have a woody flavour. Some people think that scorpion soup even has healing properties.

CASU MARZU

Care for a slice of rotting cheese? Even better, how about some rotting cheese with **maggots** inside! In Sardinia some people enjoy *casu marzu*, which means "rotten cheese." This cheese is made by allowing flies to lay their eggs in it. The eggs hatch into maggots, which feed on the cheese and make it very soft. Some people suggest wearing eye protection while eating *casu marzu*. The maggots can jump up to 15 centimetres high!

maggot *larva of some kinds of fly*

CHAPTER 4

SURPRISING SNACKS

Children around the world often like to have after-school snacks. And people of all ages get the munchies from time to time. But you may not believe how people in some countries satisfy their snack cravings!

SNACKS ON A STICK

Looking for a crunchy snack in Beijing, China? Forget about boring old crisps and biscuits. Street **vendors** here offer many strange snacks on a stick. You can choose from deep-fried cicadas, silkworm **pupae**, centipedes, scorpions, starfish or even sea horses!

vendor *person who sells something*

pupa *insect at the stage of development between a larva and an adult; more than one pupa are pupae*

FLYING ANTS

In Kenya many people eat flying white ants. Children often pick the flying ants out of the air after a rain storm. They fill buckets with the ants and eat them straight away. Kenyans also fry these ants in oil to make a crunchy snack.

HONEY ANTS

Aborigines in Australia like to snack on honey ants. They first bite down on the honey ants' abdomens, which can be as big as grapes. They then suck out the honey. People spit out the ants' bodies because they contain an acid that makes them taste bitter.

DUNG BEETLES

People around the world eat various kinds of insects. But most people think eating dung beetles is disgusting. Why? Because dung beetles feed on poo! However, some people in Thailand enjoy eating these insects. The beetles are collected from piles of water buffalo dung before being prepared for eating. Some people eat them whole. Others remove the beetles' legs and wings first. Dung beetles are said to have a crispy, nutty flavour.

STINKY TOFU

People in many parts of China love stinky **tofu**. Chefs let the tofu soak and ferment in brine for several weeks. During the fermentation process, the tofu turns black and blue and begins to stink – horribly. Just how awful is the smell? People have compared it to dog poo!

tofu *soft, cheese-like food made from soybeans*

FRIED MILK

People in Taiwan eat fried milk as a snack. You might wonder how milk can be fried. People first freeze cubes of condensed milk. The cubes are then dipped in batter before being deep-fried. The final product is crisp and chewy on the outside with a sweet, melted middle.

CAMEL CHEESE

Natives in Sudan make cheese from camel milk. They pour the milk into a skin bag and then fasten it to a camel's saddle. The milk churns and ferments in the bag as the camel moves along. Camel cheese is soft, white and creamy. It has a slightly acidic taste.

TREE GUM

Aboriginal children like to chew tree resin, or gum. The edible gum of the mulga tree is a favourite. It oozes out through the tree's bark. People sometimes shape the gum into a lump on a stick and eat it like a lollipop.

CHAPTER 5

WACKY DESSERTS AND TREATS

After a good meal, many people like to top things off with a sweet treat. In some countries, people eat ice cream that comes in outrageous flavours. In other places people love really smelly fruit. You never know what people around the world will choose for dessert!

JAPAN'S WACKY SWEETS

Almost everyone enjoys eating sweets of some kind. But in Japan sweets come in many wacky flavours. In Japanese sweet shops you can choose sweets with all sorts of flavours including octopus or sweetcorn with soy sauce. Many Japanese children also like chocolate-covered dried squid. Japanese caramels come in strange flavours too, such as black sesame, tomato, grilled lamb and even jellyfish!

CHURCHKHELA

Do you think of nuts as a type of sweet? *Churchkhela* are long strings of nuts that have been repeatedly dipped in concentrated grape juice. After each dipping, the nuts are allowed to dry. Many people in Russia, Georgia, Cyprus, Turkey and Greece enjoy this sausage-shaped sweetie.

AIS KACANG

In Singapore and Malaysia, *ais kacang* is a popular frozen treat. *Ais kacang* means "iced beans" in the Malay language. This colourful frozen treat includes red beans, sweetcorn and coloured jelly cubes. It is then topped with shaved ice, palm sugar syrup and evaporated milk. Some *ais kacang* fans enjoy chopped peanuts on top as well.

TURKISH ICE CREAM

People in Turkey call their ice cream *dondurma*. Popular flavours include pistachio and cherry. *Dondurma* is very thick and chewy. It is often eaten with a knife and fork. The key ingredient, salep, is made from orchid roots. Salep makes *dondurma* very elastic and dense so it doesn't melt too quickly.

PUERTO RICAN ICE CREAM

Ice cream lovers in Lares, Puerto Rico, can choose from many wild flavours at the Heladaría Lares restaurant. If they're feeling fishy they can choose a cone of cod or prawn ice cream. If they're in the mood for vegetables they can choose carrot or sweet potato and pumpkin ice cream. They can even select rice and bean or almond-cake ice cream. It's like having an entire meal in one cone!

MEXICAN ICE CREAM

Oaxaca, Mexico, is famous for its huge variety of wacky frozen treats. From slushy ices to iced milk, Oaxaca has it all. Popular flavours include corn, avocado, rose and even burnt milk. But the award for the strangest flavour should probably go to crispy pig-skin ice cream!

PHILIPPINO ICE CREAM

In the Philippines people often like chunks of cheese in their ice cream. One popular flavour is "vanilla with cheese." If you'd like to try some very colourful ice cream, try a scoop of *ube*. This bright purple ice cream is made from a type of yam. It's not too sweet and sometimes has coconut added to it.

DURIAN FRUIT

In Southeast Asia durian fruit is known for its strong odour. It smells so awful that it's even been banned from several hotels and from public transport. People often compare the fruit's smell to mouldy cheese, dirty socks or a city rubbish tip on a hot summer's day. But in spite of its horrid stench, some people love the way durian fruit tastes. It has a creamy flesh with a custard-like texture.

BUDDHA'S HAND FRUIT

Many Asian people also like Buddha's hand fruit. This strange citrus fruit resembles a hand with fingers. Unlike lemons or oranges, there is no juicy pulp beneath the fruit's skin. To eat raw Buddha's hand, people slice the fingers lengthways. Sometimes people use the fruit in **marmalade** or add it to stir-fry meals.

marmalade *type of jam made from citrus fruits*

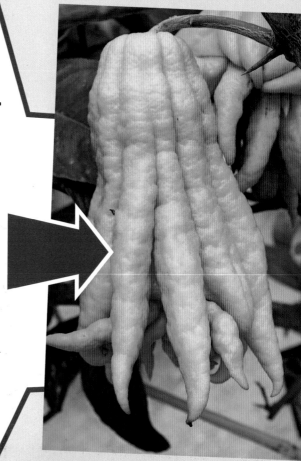

BREADFRUIT

Breadfruit is eaten throughout the Pacific Islands. When roasted in a fire, this green, lumpy fruit smells like freshly baked bread. Breadfruit is often used in cakes. It also works well in dishes to replace rice, pasta or potatoes. The taste of small breadfruit is sometimes compared to artichoke hearts.

A WORLD OF STRANGE FOOD

From Argentina to Zimbabwe, people eat all kinds of bizarre foods. Whether foods are crunchy, slimy, hairy or smelly – people somewhere on Earth love to eat them. You might find some of the foods in this book completely disgusting. But try to keep an open mind. If you're travelling in a different country, you never know which far-out food might become your new favourite!

GLOSSARY

Aborigine people who lived in Australia before European settlers arrived there

brine salty water

char type of fish similar to salmon or trout

delicacy food that is rare and considered to be especially delicious

ferment undergo a chemical change

gelatin clear substance made from bones and animal tissue

grub tiny creature that will become an insect; a larva

hominy corn kernels with the hulls removed

maggot larva of some kinds of fly

marmalade type of jam made from citrus fruits

outback huge area in the middle of Australia that is covered by deserts and rocks

pupa insect at the stage of development between a larva and an adult; more than one pupa are pupae

spit long, pointed rod that holds meat over a fire for cooking

suet hard fat from animals that is used in cooking

tofu soft, cheese-like food made from soybeans

vendor person who sells something

READ MORE

China (Country Guides with Benjamin Blog and his Inquisitive Dog), Anita Ganeri (Raintree, 2014)

Disgusting Science: A Revolting Look at What Makes Things Gross (Science Sorted), Glenn Murphy (Macmillan Children's Books, 2014)

Food (The Science Behind), Casey Rand (Raintree, 2012)

WEBSITES

www.bbc.co.uk/history/handsonhistory/romans.shtml
Travel back in time to Roman Britain to discover how the Romans changed the lives of people living here, including some of their food choices!

www.foodafactoflife.org.uk
Explore this website and learn more about foods from around the world. Play interactive games and help the characters to make healthy food choices.

www.roughguides.com/gallery/weird-food
Go to this website to see some amazing photographs and read some interesting descriptions of some very strange food from around the world.

INDEX